T0198660

Teachable Moments

Teachable Moments

Lessons from Africa

Hank Wagner

iUniverse, Inc.
New York Bloomington

Teachable Moments
Lessons from Africa

Copyright © 2009 Hank Wagner

iUniverse books may be ordered through booksellers or by contacting:

iUniverse
1663 Liberty Drive
Bloomington, IN 47403
www.iuniverse.com
1-800-Authors (1-800-288-4677)

ISBN: 978-1-4401-9077-3 (pbk)
ISBN: 978-1-4401-9078-0 (ebook)

Printed in the United States of America

iUniverse rev. date: 11.18.09

Dedication

Without my wonderful wife, Pam, this book could never have happened. She is always there, through good times and bad, and she never allows me to even consider giving up. We have been married more than twenty-six years, and I can't imagine what my life might be like without her. She is an awesome wife and an incredible mother.

Pam and I are the proud parents of two awesome children. They have made being a parent one of the most rewarding things in my life. I am very proud of both of them and would not trade the experience of being a dad for anything. Shawn and Laura both have huge potential, and it is exciting to watch their lives unfold. Shawn and Laura, I believe in you.

This book could also never have happened without Dan Fielder. Organizing the trip to Africa was only the beginning of his contribution to my life; he has changed how I see the world. He taught me many life lessons that not only come through in this book, but are also deeply embedded in the daily lives of my family.

Kevin Kallies was my closest partner in Africa. He offered a constant reminder of how laughter can change almost every situation for the better. We witnessed many challenges in Africa, and his laughter not only carried us through, but also touched the life of almost everyone Kevin met. Chapter 30 is dedicated to him.

And finally, I owe a debt of gratitude to my dear friend Shelly Mayer; she has motivated me to push myself to my limits many, many, times. She is a great judge of character and when she sees potential in people, she continues to pull them toward it. The trip to Africa happened five years ago, and if not for Shelly's constant encouragement, it may never have been put into a book.

Contents

Introduction

In early March of 2004, I had the opportunity to spend ten days in Togo, Africa. A mentor of mine had recently told me that all great men and women make a habit of doing something bigger than themselves. He also encouraged me to think beyond my own little corner of the world. So I chose Africa, for a few reasons, as a place to serve and to do something beyond myself.

Few days have passed since that I have not thought about my experiences during my life-changing stay in Africa. I often find myself thinking about what the African people are doing at that very moment halfway around the globe. I wish I could have done more for the people of Africa. It appears, at least at this time, that Africa has done more for me than I have done for her.

After returning from Africa, I found myself continually looking at my diary that I had kept and my list of lessons that I had learned. I had shared these discoveries with very few people and could not seem to get rid of the small, still voice telling me to share them with others. Experience has taught me that when a thought or desire to take action comes from within and won't go away, we should just do it!

So every Monday morning for fifty-two weeks, I e-mailed a "Lesson from Africa" to a small list of people. I sent them weekly so that the reader could spend seven days thinking about the lesson and how it might apply to them before being allowed to read the next lesson.

As you read this book, I would encourage you to follow a similar process. If you do not want to wait a week between chapters, at least allow yourself one day to think about what you read and allow that chapter to impact your life before you move on to the next one. And who knows—you may need a chance in between chapters to call and talk to someone you love, or maybe order some flowers to show them that you care. I encourage you to share some of these lessons with your family. You and your children may never see Africa, but that does not mean that a small part of Africa cannot come to you.

One of the desired outcomes of this book is to positively influence people. We are the most important thing on this planet, and our importance has little to do with where we live or the things that we own. Everyone, including people in the poorest parts of Africa, have greatness within themselves. Hopefully this book allows Africa to touch your life as it has mine.

Chapter One

You Are Important to Me

Today, on March 1, 2004, my three travel companions and I are within minutes of leaving for Togo, Africa. Most of our loved ones are crying. These three men and I are not headed to war, and we will only be gone for ten days. Why are they crying or feeling sad?

The place where we are going has its dangers, but I believe that their tears are not expressing fear. I believe they are saying, "You are important to me." I believe that each person carrying a tear in their eye was showing a deep, heartfelt appreciation for the relationship they were about to lose, even if only for a short time.

We all see those same tears as brave men and women leave for military assignments. At every funeral, those same tears are falling, sending the same message: "You are important to me."

Why is this heartfelt thankfulness for our relationships not a part of our daily life? Why are we not really thankful for a person until he or she is lost?

Before going to the next chapter, force yourself to examine how you relate to others. Who are you taking for granted? As you speak, listen to yourself for signs of gratitude in the words that you are speaking to others. As you spend time with others, ask yourself what life would be like without them. What have they contributed to your life, and are they aware of your thankfulness toward them?

Hopefully this will inspire some creative ideas on how to show your thanks and appreciation for them now, not just when they're about to leave you. And if nothing else, maybe the simple words "thank you" or "you are important to me" will leave your lips more often.

Your words have the power to bring love, respect, appreciation, value, honor, and so on. Please choose them wisely this week as you value the people around you.

Chapter Two

You Are Important to Me—Part II

If one word could sum up my feelings after my experience in Africa, it would have to be "thankful." In the last chapter, you were encouraged to think about relationships and how important they are to you. This chapter is an expansion of that.

As my travel companions and I drove to the airport in Chicago, one of the men recounted a gesture he had made before leaving town. He had gone to a local flower shop and left some important instructions with the employees. He gave the florists a special card or letter that they were to attach to some flowers and send out each day that he would be in Africa.

For the next ten days, he would be thousands of miles away, with no telephone or other means of communication. But each and every day, he would touch the life of another person back home.

True gratitude is a state of mind—or heart. Thankfulness is not something to be experienced only when something good happens to us; we choose it regardless of what is happening around us. Thankfulness should always be in action in our lives. And effort and planning are often required to express this gratitude.

In the last chapter, you were encouraged to think about the value of people as you spoke with them. You were also instructed to listen to yourself and to choose words that would express your gratitude to people around you.

Now I would like you to go beyond words. Think bigger. Words are very important, but now let's turn our thankfulness into action. Send flowers or a handwritten card. Before going on to the next chapter, stop and take some time to reflect. Then think about how you can appreciate, value, or thank some of the people around you. Make it a lifestyle to recognize the good in others and to regularly thank them. The world will be a much better place if everyone is thankful for each other, and that vision must start with us.

Chapter Three

America the Beautiful

Once we arrived at the airport in Chicago, we had our final meal at McDonald's and found the gate where we were to board our plane. But something was very wrong.

I have been in airports many times, but something was very different and very wrong here. Yes, most of the people were black and spoke a different language than I, but it was something bigger than that.

People were very quiet, even somber, and it seemed as if everyone was in a state of shock. They would just sit and stare off in the distance, as if something were really bothering them. We did not witness this anywhere else in the airport; this unusual atmosphere was only at this gate.

Most of my airport experience has come from vacations my family has taken. The planes usually were full of smiling people whose hearts were bursting with joy and expectation. On every other plane I had been on, people usually had extra bags filled with possessions and snacks to take on the plane with them ... but not at this gate. No bags and no excitement—but why?

It then really started to sink in: this was no vacation. I did not fully realize the extent of these passengers' feelings until my return from Africa. Those people *were* in shock. Most of those people waiting to board that plane were preparing to return home, to a place I had not yet seen or experienced. Those people had just experienced one of the most advanced, prosperous, and blessed nations in the world.

Their shock was not just a result of America's abundance and opportunity. Their shock also came from the knowledge that the American lifestyle was something they could never have, in a place they would never be allowed to live. Imagine the sorrow you might feel after seeing all of the wonderful blessings this country has to offer, then realizing that you could never bring your family here, instead remaining confined to poverty.

Be thankful you were born in this country. Never speak against her. I do not know why I was born here instead of Africa, but I can assure you of this: I will not live another day without being thankful for America. America is filled with people who do not realize how blessed we are. If you know someone who does not have a heartfelt thankfulness for our country, I can promise you that a visit to the remote areas of Africa will give it to them.

One of the goals of this book is to help people realize all that they have to be thankful for. I was not aware of the many blessings I took for granted until I visited Africa. By the end of this book, hopefully you will also be able to recognize some of those gifts and become willing to do your part to inoculate the rest of our country with thankfulness.

Chapter Four

Homesick Already

After eighteen hours in flight, I landed in Africa with a much better understanding of jet lag. My companions and I felt physically drained but somewhat excited to finally reach our destination.

Our plane had come to a stop on the runway—just waiting for clearance to the terminal, I thought. Instead they were unloading us right there. I was looking forward to meeting new people and excited to try to make a difference during my stay. As I exited the plane, I am sure my enthusiastic expression was replaced with a much different one—a look that stayed with me the entire trip. It was that same look that I had seen on those passengers returning to Africa from America: one of shock and unbelief.

It was late at night, and as we walked out of the plane, it was hard to see much farther than one hundred yards. Our plane had stopped far from any buildings, and the lighting was very limited. We walked down the plane's exit stairs, much as the president of the United States does when exiting his private jet. But at the bottom of the stairs, the celebrity fantasy immediately stopped.

Security was slim, almost nonexistent. No well-dressed people directed us to a baggage claim or welcomed us to their country. People were scrambling to find a place on two old buses that had pulled up. We followed, assuming they were headed to the terminal.

This so-called terminal was like nothing I had ever seen before. It was a single-story building that was about forty feet wide and eighty feet long. There were no stairs, no escalators, no air conditioning, and limited lighting. The building had few interior walls, just makeshift wood-and-cloth partitions to guide us through. It was an immediate wake-up call for me, and I found myself quickly wondering if this visit was really a good idea.

After forty-five minutes, we had made it through security. I could not feel any sense of the usual "welcome to our country" sentiment that I was accustomed to receiving in every other place I had been. Instead I felt a strong anger or jealousy toward me. As we passed through the airport and I had to look into the eyes of every person, it made me want to go home even more.

I had thought every country understood the value of tourism and the money it brings to local businesses. And we were not just tourists; our motivation for being among these people was to see if we could in some way help them. I could not understand why they did not seem happy to see us.

Once again, be thankful for where you live. In future chapters, you will see why those people that I met for the first time in Africa that dark and scary night were not very happy to see us—and for some of those reasons, I can't blame them.

--------- *Chapter Five* ---------

The Oscars

As we neared the end of airport security, we were excited to see Pastor Charles waiting for us. This pastor from Togo, Africa, would be our host during our stay.

He welcomed us and then helped us locate our luggage. As we moved toward the exit of the terminal, Pastor Charles asked me to follow closely behind the gentlemen carrying our luggage. He also instructed me to watch them very closely. I did not find out until later that it was so they would not steal all that we had.

As we stepped single file out of the terminal, something very strange happened. I instantly felt as if we were exiting a time machine and were now in the Oscars!

There was no red carpet, no movie cameras, and no TV crews, only a narrow roped-off trail made with some posts and rope. On each side were people, seemingly hundreds of them. Many of them were just like people at the Oscars—there just to watch. Those people looked at me as I have never been looked at before.

Time seemed to go into slow motion, and I felt each of their eyes lock on to us as we walked by. They have few televisions in the part of Africa that we were in, and most of them only show very, very, old black-and-white American shows. These people had no idea what the Oscars were, but I felt like a celebrity. Their faces were clearly saying, "Why couldn't that be me?" As I walked down this winding trail, this revelation became entrenched in my heart. As I slowly passed by each person, and my eyes connected with theirs, it felt as if their eyes were begging for an answer to this question. *How can I have what you have?*

I was unsure if I should feel thankful, sorry, guilty, sad, happy, or just plain scared. But one thing I was sure of: I had just experienced a very important life lesson, one that was branded into my heart and impossible to ever block out or forget.

You, most likely, would also be looked upon as a king or queen in Africa—and probably ninety percent of the world. We must not take for granted the blessings we have around us. And we must not be arrogant and think that we earned them or somehow deserve them, because we could have been born in Africa!

Before going to the next chapter, start a list of some of the blessings around you. Put it on the refrigerator or near the dinner table. Get your family involved in adding to this list daily. Maybe at every meal as you and your family give thanks, think of one more thing that you are blessed with and add it to the list. See how long you can go or how long that list will get before you run out of things to be truly thankful for.

Chapter Six

Give Thanks for Food

After driving for a couple hours, we would soon get our first meal in Africa. We drove to our hotel in Ghana, where we would spend the night before leaving for Togo in the morning. It was dark, and there were no streetlights or lighted signs to help get a feel for where we were going or what the surroundings were like. We could not see or hear anything, but I was sure that what we were passing was not what tourists would pay to see.

Before we left America, we had visited a physician who not only vaccinated us, but also gave us numerous instructions. Among them was, "Be very careful what you eat." He told us to stay away from anything that had not been cooked thoroughly to remove harmful bacteria.

After he had gone through the list of things that could go wrong from eating the wrong food while in Africa, I can assure you the thought of backing out of the trip did cross my mind. And I had many so-called friends who also encouraged me with grim ideas of what our diet would be like.

As you can probably see, when it came to food, I expected the worst. My first meal on the plane already had me missing my wife, Pam. She is a farm girl and has always believed that at least one meal a day should be meat, potatoes, and vegetables. And her mom always told her that a good cook should never run out of food. Yes, I admit that I am spoiled, and I suspect that many of you reading this book are as well. But, like me, you may not realize how thankful we should be for something until it is taken from us.

My first meal in Africa was in the hotel restaurant and consisted of chicken and pasta. It may have been the worst chicken I ever had, but it was still great compared to what I expected. We had just eaten in one of the finest restaurants in the area and maybe had the best meal we would see for ten days.

I lived mostly on bread and fruit while in Africa. The bread was great, and the fruit was awesome. We were staying near the west coast of Africa, and fruit was abundant. There were many pineapple trees in the area, and that fruit went right from the tree to our table; it was the best pineapple I had ever eaten.

Thankfully, our host took great care of us, and we did not have to eat to survive like most people we met. These people don't think about what they would like to eat and then pick a restaurant. They don't go to a local grocery store to choose their food to feed their families. They have no refrigerators or freezers to store their food, and even if they did, there is no electricity to run them. And as you might guess, meat, fish, and many other foods turn ugly very quickly with temperatures consistently above ninety degrees.

I am not going to go into detail about some of the food that I saw eaten out of respect for the people of Africa. You and I would eat those things too, if that was all we had to keep ourselves and our children alive.

I am not sure if we can really become thankful for something just by someone telling us that we should be. My parents always had our family give thanks at every meal for our food, but it was not until my trip to Africa that I truly became thankful for it. After my trip to Africa, I have a low tolerance for people who refuse to be thankful. My children have heard many, many, many times about why they should be more thankful for their food.

But it was probably the time they went without that sent the message home.

It was a Sunday afternoon, and quite often on such afternoons, we would go somewhere to eat following church. It was a chance to give Pam a break from cooking and a chance for our family to eat out as well. We would usually talk about where we would eat and often spent this time with another family. It was something that we always looked forward to.

But on this day, as we drove out of the parking lot, I turned toward home.

"Dad, you are going the wrong way," Laura pointed out from the backseat. I proceeded to tell them about how the people I spent time with in Africa usually had only one meal per day, and that it was often only a piece of bread. I informed them that we would not only be going right home, but that we would be skipping our meal altogether. By the end of the day, they had a much better understanding of what I was trying to tell them about being more thankful for the food we have to eat.

As you go to the grocery store this week, or sit down at your table to eat, realize that in Africa, and many other parts of the world, people are starving at this very moment.

--------- *Chapter Seven* ---------

Thankful for the EPA

As daylight came upon us, I hurried to the window of our hotel to get my first glimpse of Africa. The window faced outward from the rear of our hotel, and I did not see anything unusual ... well, other than the armed guard pacing the parking lot with a machine gun! Those men with machine guns were not for looks, and they were not afraid to use their weapons. After the less-than-appreciative welcome at the airport I was not sure if they were there to protect us or to keep us out. You will see in another chapter what the role of those men with guns is and how their way of enforcing the law is much different than ours.

After loading up our belongings and departing the comfort and security of our hotel, we began our adventure in Africa. We were in Accra, the capital of Ghana and home to approximately 750,000 people.

At every street corner, people would literally surround the cars trying to sell things. Most were young children, and they were selling everything you could imagine. Some were very old items like old, unpopular music CDs from the United States. What made this really unusual is that few, if any, people had a CD player. Those CDs were likely someone's gift to them that they were now trying to sell so they could buy things to survive.

Vehicles were abundant in this city. I did feel once again as if I had exited a time machine, because every vehicle was very old. I don't think I saw one less than twenty years old. Every vehicle was extremely overloaded, either with people or supplies. They did not have money to go cruising, but had a purpose behind every mile.

The air was thick, humid, and filled with the smell of exhaust and burning oil. Not only were the vehicles very old, but also the quality of their gas and oil was very poor. Dark black exhaust was common on over half of the cars and all of the trucks.

This may seem odd, but I have a new appreciation for our Environmental Protection Agency. Yes, we live in a country with many rules and regulations, and that is often the source of many complaints. But most, if not all, of our rules and regulations are for our benefit. Our air is fresh and clean, and I can assure you that I will never complain about regulations again without thoroughly assessing what it would be like without them.

Chapter Eight

Potholes Everywhere

As we were leaving Accra on our first morning in Africa, I commented to one of the guys that this was not as bad as I had expected. Our driver assured us that we had not yet seen Africa. He said that we were in a city that would compare to our Chicago or maybe New York. He also explained that we had just seen the prosperous people.

We left the city, and I started to understand what he meant. Our blacktop road had now turned into a dirt one with huge potholes—not just an occasional one, but literally thousands of them. The next two hours of travel consisted of a constant swerving to avoid them.

People from both directions were going from one side of the road to another trying to avoid them. These were not your typical American potholes; they were wide and very deep. Many had the power to swallow an entire vehicle in one encounter!

Our speed ranged from zero to twenty-five miles per hour. No need for a speed limit; the potholes took care of that. There were no road signs to warn of the holes or any other obstacles.

Yes, we have taxes in America, but we also have absolutely fabulous roads, and we have road crews that monitor their condition twenty-four hours a day, seven days a week. I have been guilty of complaining about road construction—never again. I have been a party to the numerous jokes targeting our road crews—never again.

Many times since returning from Africa I have thanked our township and our county for the time, money, and effort they put into the care of our roads.

By the way, I did ask our driver why those roads in Africa were not being repaired, and that is next chapter's lesson.

Chapter Nine

Honesty, Integrity, and Government

"Why are there no crews out fixing these roads?" I asked our driver. His answer astonished me.

"First of all," he said, "there is no money. And the main reason that there is no money is because our government is very corrupt."

He went on to explain that many countries have sent money to Africa to help improve the roads. Other countries have recognized the need for good transportation to develop and prosper a nation. I felt proud as he told us the road we were driving on was funded in part by America. Yes, the road was full of potholes, but it was still better than no road at all.

He went on to further describe the corruptness of their government. He sadly admitted that it is very hard to get anything to the people of Africa. The government is free to open and inspect all things coming into the country and regularly takes whatever they wish.

The African people have no elections, and the only option is to fight and try to overthrow whoever is in power. But not only do the people not have any weapons, but also no means of transportation or communication. They are held somewhat captive to the corruption that leads them.

Our government is not perfect by any means, but I believe it is one to be thankful for. The freedom and structure that our forefathers fought for and designed is one to be proud of. I will be very slow to say anything negative about our government or our nation's road crews ever again!

Chapter Ten

Spiritual Battles

This two-hour car ride to Togo was like a roller-coaster ride, both physically and mentally. We had been in Africa less than twenty-four hours, and it seemed as if my every emotion had been tapped.

Gradually, we found our way into an area that brought me hope and encouragement. Some of the most beautiful woodwork that I had ever seen was lined up along the road we were traveling on. It began with beds, chairs, tables, and then doors. Knowing that it was all made with primitive hand tools made these works of art even more astonishing to me.

No power tools of any kind had been used, because there was no electricity. There were also no buildings or workshops; the work was all being done outside. During this time, there was no rain or humidity to worry about, only the very hot temperatures.

As we continued our journey toward Togo, the emotional roller-coaster took a turn down once again. Almost as if it were a transition to something worse, an area appeared outside our windows that seemed like miles of wood coffins. All of them were designed like the coffins seen on the old western TV shows. Some were rectangular and some were somewhat diamond-shaped, but all were just plain, simple, unpainted wood. Don't get me wrong, same amazing quality, just not what I wanted to see!

It seemed as if people with common gifts or beliefs tended to settle in one area. Following the coffins, we entered realm of the next eye-opener: voodoo. There were not only unusual things at these places, but you could just feel the evil as we passed through this area. I don't know where your spiritual beliefs are, but I saw evil like I have never seen evil before. We were still in the comfort of our vehicle, but I wondered what we would do if we had problems with our car in this area.

Be thankful that you were born in a country that was formed by men and women who were willing to take a stand for good and not evil. Be thankful that many people have been willing to give their lives to stand for good and fight evil.

We live in a blessed country, and I for one am quite thankful God is in it. And if you have a hard time believing in the forces of good and evil, Africa will show you the extremes of both.

Chapter Eleven

The Border

Finally we reached the border to the next country and our final destination: Togo. Our escort told us to stay in the car—no pictures and no unusual incidents. He was not joking with us and seemed somewhat stern about his orders. He left with our passports and other papers that hopefully would allow us to proceed. He walked into a relatively small building with armed guards standing on each side of the doorway. There were also other men with assault rifles in the area; they were not smiling, and the atmosphere was not bringing joy and excitement.

Upon his return, our driver informed us that those armed guards had the power to do just about anything with us. They could put us in one of their jails and lose track of us—or worse, shoot us on the spot for whatever reason they felt necessary. It was really starting to sink in: *We are not in Kansas anymore, Toto.*

We went through many checkpoints like this while in Africa. I don't know if I was ever so happy to have a pastor with me. Pastors have huge clout in Africa. I think it comes mainly from the realization of the strong battle between good and evil that is very apparent.

The government there understands the tough job that pastors have, and that they regularly fight for good. The people and the government have seen firsthand what evil left unchecked can do, and they place great value on their spiritual leaders. We should not be any different. Please tell your pastor, minister, or priest thank you, and that you appreciate them as well.

Come on, step out of the box a little and make that call now. It will only take five minutes, and you might really make their day. And if you don't have someone whom you look up to as a spiritual leader, then look in the yellow pages and pick one. You have nothing to lose by taking a few minutes to thank them for what they do.

---------------- *Chapter Twelve* ----------------

Use Your Head

One sight that was quite common was something that I had seen in the movies, but I always thought it was not real. I thought that people were not really foolish enough to carry things on their heads.

But in Africa, people really do carry almost everything on their heads. When I first saw this, I immediately thought that I was much smarter than they were, and that I should teach them how to carry something. Thankfully, humility took over, and I shut my mouth and observed.

First of all, I noticed that all African people had incredible posture. Carrying things on their heads required them to walk straight and tall. It also gave them incredible skill related to balance and coordination. And I am sure that patience had to be developed in there somewhere.

I have never seen anyone in America ever carry anything on his or her head. But in Africa, I saw every thing from a small bowl of fruit to a refrigerator being carried up top. Some of the things people were carrying were bigger than they were, yet they carried them with ease. Think about how the load is being evenly distributed on our bodies. Could it be that they have one up on us here?

If you were to visit our farm, would you see us carrying bales of hay on our heads? Probably not, but I will say this: many times (okay, most times) when I think that I am right or that I have the answer, I have found that it is best to be quiet, listen, and be continually amazed at what I can learn.

———————— *Chapter Thirteen* ————————

Don't Do It

I have learned a tremendous amount from Africa, but there are some things that I would like to teach the people in Africa—or at least things that I would not want to have my children do at home. This chapter's lesson or experience recounts one of them. I will share it with you, and then you decide.

I rarely saw a bathroom during my stay in Africa. I will admit that the first time that I saw why they don't have many bathrooms, I did a double take. When they have to go, they just stop walking and … go! Yes, it appeared that any time, and any place, was okay.

The amazing thing about it is that they have always done it that way and therefore see nothing wrong with it. I wonder how many things we are doing simply because it has always been done that way.

Is it wrong? They don't have money for food or clothing. They do not have many of the small things that we regularly take for granted, and in many cases they do not even have a home to place a bathroom in. If we had been born there, we would likely do the very same thing. So today, and for the rest of your life, every time you go to the bathroom, be thankful. And as you are sitting there, try to remember those people less fortunate than you. You could have been born in Africa.

——————— *Chapter Fourteen* ———————

Opportunity

I love the word "opportunity." Better yet, I love what it represents: a chance to improve things, a chance to have a better outcome, a chance to positively influence a life. Africa could be seen as a place of tremendous challenge or a place filled with opportunities yet to be discovered.

Today I would have a challenge—or, I should say, potential opportunity. Each of the four of us who went to Africa had been asked to teach at a college there, and today was my day.

It was not this huge campus with thousands of students. It was a small building with fifteen to twenty students. Few people in Africa have the chance to finish high school, much less think about college. Many different languages are spoken in Africa, and it took two interpreters to speak to this group of students.

I did not sleep much the night before, and my roommate asked me why. I told him that I take the responsibility of speaking to people very seriously. He countered with, "These people are in Africa, and you will probably never see them again." Exactly—my life would only be connected to theirs for a short period of time. What could I tell them that would make the best use of that precious time? I found myself wondering if I should talk at all or just listen.

I talked to them about the importance of leadership. I tried to help them see how important they were in determining not only their individual future but the direction of their families and country as well. Each of them has a purpose, and they must be determined to find and fulfill that purpose. I wanted to help them see how each of them could in many ways impact the lives of others in a positive way even in the poorest parts of Africa.

I believe in divine appointments. I believe that people are the most important thing on this planet. I believe that what makes each day successful is tied to the impact had on the life of another person.

Those students were very respectful, listening to every word that was spoken. I may never know if any of those lives were changed that day, but the thought of possibly influencing a life halfway around the world was both exciting and rewarding for me. Who knows—a future leader of Africa could have been in that room.

No matter where you are today, I am quite sure that you are surrounded with opportunity. It may be a chance to learn something or possibly change a habit. It might be something as simple as changing how you think or becoming more thankful, or it could be touching the life of another. Something as simple as a smile or an enthusiastic "good morning" may be all it takes to impact the life of another in a positive way.

Before going on to the next chapter, force yourself to find and capitalize on opportunity. Become an opportunity hunter, and make sure that it includes touching the lives of others.

—————————— *Chapter Fifteen* ——————————

Where Do You Sleep?

It was 4:00 AM in Africa, and we were to take part in an early morning radio broadcast. Radio is the primary means of communication in Africa; television is almost nonexistent. We were asked to accompany our host as he did his regular morning broadcast. We did not know that we would be asked to be a part of his broadcast—challenge or opportunity?

Our driver was low on gas and pulled into a gas station. It was almost completely dark; streetlights were few and far between. The only thing that remotely resembled our gas stations was two very old gas pumps. They were very plain, basic pumps, with no slots for credit card and no digital readouts.

The place was completely dark except for the headlights of our vehicle. Our driver beeped his horn, and nothing happened. I was wondering why he was beeping his horn; the place was obviously closed. He honked once again—another, somewhat longer beep this time—and to my amazement, less than ten feet away, a man got up from his sleep to come and pump our gas.

As we drove through town, I saw people sleeping outside everywhere. They were lying on the ground, and when I say ground, I mean ground. Why were these people sleeping outside and not inside their homes or in their beds?

"First of all," he answered, "nobody has air-conditioning, and it is much cooler outside. Second, many of these people do not have beds. And third, some don't have homes to put beds in!"

Before you go to sleep tonight, go outside and find a patch of bare ground—please, not on the grass, because there is no grass to sleep on in Togo, Africa. If you have a family, take them all outside and broaden their understanding of the world they live in. Lie down and imagine yourself sleeping in that place for the rest of your life.

I don't believe that we should feel guilty for the things that we have, but I do believe that being thankful is extremely important. Someone very wise once told me this: "The things in your life that you are thankful for will multiply, and the things that you are not thankful for will slowly exit your life."

––––––––––––––– *Chapter Sixteen* –––––––––––––––

Motor Scooters Everywhere

By 6:00 AM, I had discovered that the radio program was like everything else so far: quite enlightening. We thought that we were just there to accompany our host while he did his daily radio program. Then he introduced us and told us to speak to the people of Togo. We were not prepared for that, but sometimes opportunities come and go very quickly.

Afterward, we found ourselves sitting at an intersection in the middle of Lomé, a city of more than seven hundred thousand people. There were very few traffic laws and very few signs; everyone just seemed to know what to do. Sometimes a picture would take the place of a thousand words, and this was one of those times. If only I would have remembered my camera that morning.

There must have been a hundred scooters lined up in front of us. No, they were not on some benefit motorcycle ride. Other than walking, this was the main form of transportation. These people were not out joyriding; they did not have money to spend this way, so there was purpose behind every trip. Almost every scooter had two people, and many were being used like taxis to transport people.

Imagine having scooters constitute 75 percent of the traffic in any of our large cities. Take away the stoplights and the street signs. We would need a policeman at every corner, or there would be major chaos. I am sure that people would be killing each other, and travel would not be possible.

For more on what makes this possible in Togo, Africa, see the next chapter.

————— *Chapter Seventeen* —————

Attitude Is Everything

The city of Lomé, where we were staying had 750,000 people! This was almost impossible to imagine without skyscrapers or any large buildings. There were no transit systems or other means of mass transportation.

The roads were all dirt (which is the next chapter's topic) and were in very poor condition. There were literally hundreds of scooters going all directions. Mix in with that cars, bikes, and people. In America, if we tried to duplicate this, we would have murders at every street corner.

During my entire stay in Lomé, Africa, I never once saw any strife, anger, or frustration directed toward another person. At least a hundred times, I saw a driver cut in front of another or pull some stunt that would have earned him a long horn beep and some choice words back home.

I was appalled at how this could be and asked for an explanation. Our host explained that the people of Togo would always immediately forgive anyone who did something against them. Even if the other person is totally wrong, they will not carry any feelings of anger or unforgiveness.

You could see it in their faces and in their actions. It was an almost unexplainable kindness, compassion, and love toward others. Our host went on to explain that that was why a corrupt government had been allowed to stay in power over thirty years.

The people are not fighters, but compassionate and caring toward others. Not only are the streets always full of people, but also there is intense spiritual conflict like I have never seen before. Yet I never saw anyone fighting, pushing, or even yelling at another person.

If there were anything that I could somehow bring back and implant in the people of America, it would be this. It seems that there is no pill or injection that will accomplish this goal. It appears that it will need to be done through developing and training people, one person at a time.

Will you be one of those people?

———————— *Chapter Eighteen* ————————

What Will They Be Like When It Rains?

As I mentioned earlier in the book, we started our trip from the airport in Ghana, Africa, on poor quality concrete, then blacktop, and now dirt. In Lomé, there were no sidewalks, no curbs, and no paving or even gravel on the streets—no gutters, ditches, or rainwater-collection system.

Granted, it had not rained in over six months and would likely not rain for another month. The only real current problem was the dust—well, and the huge holes, ruts, washouts, and numerous other things left from last year's rainy season.

I kid you not, any of my plowed fields would be a treat compared to these streets. How could they put up with this? Why didn't they at least grade them level? What would happen when the rainy season came and it rained for a month straight? The soil was very poor and packed quite hard. Even though it was extremely dry, it would not soak up water quickly. As I said earlier, there was nothing in place to channel water away. Where would they sleep then? How would scooters or cars move?

Part of the reason they put up with it is because of the laid-back, forgiving attitude of the people. Okay, maybe there is a time to stand up and say, "Something needs to be done here!" Could this be a clue to what they may need to do to exit poverty?

Then I found out that the United States had sent over large sums of money to completely pave the streets of this city. It was starting to look like maybe this laid-back and forgiving attitude was not *always* right.

The condition of these streets was very frustrating and saddening to me. I wanted to call home and have my pay loader loaded on a ship and sent over. I would fix these roads myself. Then it occurred to me that my loader would be confiscated at the port it arrived in by the government.

Once again, we have no idea how blessed we really are and how thankful we need to be.

Chapter Nineteen

Green Grass

My wife, Pam, loves green grass. Nothing seems to give her more pleasure than a well-groomed, bright green lawn. Somehow even on her bad days just cutting the grass brings a smile to her face.

Okay, I admit that I sometimes tease Pam about her love for a well-groomed lawn. But Pam, I am very thankful for all you do to keep our farm looking so nice. And while in Africa, I gained new appreciation for the ability to have a nice, green lawn.

During my time in Africa, I did not see any green grass; it was all dirt. There were some trees growing in the city but not one blade of grass. Maybe during the rainy season there would be some grass, and that would only be for a short time.

But on the morning we returned from the radio station, I saw something along the way that immediately made me think of Pam. There was a lady out in front of her home with a branch that was broken off of some tree. It was about eighteen inches long and a foot wide.

She was using it like a rake or broom to groom the dirt around her home! She had no green grass and would likely never see any. Her home was smaller than most ice shacks. The floors were dirt, and it had no doors or windows.

Yet she found joy and satisfaction in caring for what she had. Seeing that take place not only made me think of Pam but brought me a sense of hope and thankfulness. Even with the poverty that was all around, this lady was thankful for what she had. How could I know that without the chance to meet her or learn about what was important to her?

You will take care of what you are thankful for and neglect those things that you are not thankful for. Whether the possession in question is cars, grass, or even people, you can tell the level of thankfulness by how people care for them.

I want to be a person who is always thankful. I want to be around people who are always thankful. I wish to influence, encourage, and train people to be more thankful. Can you help? Will you help? And if so, how will you help?

--------- *Chapter Twenty* ---------

Each Country an Island

Africa is our second-largest continent, and it contains 23 percent of the world's total land area. The continent of Africa also contains 53 different countries. Each country is like its own little world. Each country has its own system of money. And to convert our money to theirs takes nothing short of a miracle.

Even though rules and regulations are somewhat limited, laws are also very different from one country to another, and that will be the subject for another chapter.

The culture is very different in every country. Because the residents of each country cannot travel very far, and they have little contact with the outside world, many old traditions remain, both good and bad. The culture in Togo was one that was relatively safe to live in. It was strongly recommended that we not go to Nigeria. The people there would kill you for your car or cut your arm off to get your watch.

When we travel to other states here in America, we can often detect an accent—but at least we all speak the same language. There is some debate as to how many languages are spoken in Africa. Most experts have placed the number somewhere between two thousand and three thousand different languages. The most common seems to be Swahili, but many Africans can speak three or four other languages. How does that make you feel—that they have very limited education, and yet they are able to speak multiple languages?

In Ghana and Togo, where we spent all of our time, French was quite common. I asked why and was told that those two countries were overthrown and ruled by the French for many years. Many other African countries were also conquered and ruled by European nations.

I could not understand why anyone would fight for control of this desolate land. So I asked, and in the next chapter, you will get some of the somewhat surprising answers.

─────── *Chapter Twenty-One* ───────

Land of Opportunity?

What could all those European countries see that I am not seeing? As we drove through the countryside, better known as "the bush," I could not imagine (with all due respect) why anyone would want to conquer this land.

The fields were dry and barren. The soil looked as if it could not support anything other than a few plants. And the little vegetation that was there was being burned; smoke was everywhere. "Why are you burning the little vegetation that you have?" I asked.

They were preparing for the rainy season and a small chance to grow something for their families to eat. They had nothing with which to kill weeds, so they burned everything before the rainy season came. It was not a hot fire that quickly swept across the landscape, but a smoldering fire that lasted at least a month. Imagine extremely hot temperatures, no air conditioning or buildings to hide in, and all of the air that you see, feel, and breathe for a month being saturated with smoke.

It was definitely not fertile soil that lured the Europeans to conquer this land. Our guide then asked us to look around and see what was being sold in the markets: gold, gold, and more gold! There were primitive shops everywhere that were working with gold as if it was wood. They would hammer and shape pure gold into precious items right before our eyes. Could that be what the Europeans were after?

Africa not only has gold, but also is one of the world's richest sources of diamonds and other precious metals. Africa also contains significant oil reserves, and ivory was also a tremendous draw for Europeans. So as you can see there were many reasons for greed-stricken leaders to fight for their share of Africa.

One other resource may have been even larger and more valuable than gold and precious metals in the eyes of foreign leaders. That will be the next chapter's lesson from Africa.

—————— *Chapter Twenty-Two* ——————

Now I Understand

Our host promised us some sightseeing and a chance to see a little more of his country. And once again, the day was almost overwhelming as I saw and heard more about the history of this nation.

We drove along the west coast of Africa, we observed bright sunshine, warm temperatures, and the calming sound of the ocean's waves crashing against the shore. I have seen a few ocean beaches, but never have I experienced any like this one. Some of what I saw will be revealed in future chapters, but I can assure you, this beach was not filled with tourists swimming and tanning.

"What is that huge pier for?" we asked. It was probably 50 feet wide and at least 500 feet long. Its construction was extremely rugged, and it looked as if it had not been used in a while.

It was almost as if our guide had hoped we wouldn't see it. We asked again what the pier was for and then waited through another period of some silence before he finally told us that it was used for a train. I thought they would be proud of its construction and how this train allowed them to both import and export.

We were so intrigued by this huge pier that we wanted to know more. I was not ready for what he proceeded to tell us: that pier was mainly used for export. And the goods that were exported from that pier were what many European rulers saw as Africa's greatest resource.

That train would come off huge boats onto this pier and travel a very short distance to another equally large building to load its cargo. This cargo was not goods manufactured in factories that were proudly being exported to other countries. It was not crops grown or valuable resources mined from the ground and sold to help feed and clothe the people of Africa.

The cargo regularly leaving that pier was human beings destined for slavery. Millions and millions of young African men and boys were taken from their homes and families and herded like cattle into slavery. The men and boys were packed into ships so tight that a third of them died before reaching their destination.

Now I have a better understanding of why some of the people of Africa are not excited about tourists. Imagine yourself never seeing your grandfather or hearing the heart-wrenching stories of loved ones being captured and forced onto a ship, never to be seen again. How would you feel looking into the eyes of people who come from a country that did this to your loved ones? Now I understand the lack of "welcome to our country" at the airport. Africa was robbed, and some of that human loot was shipped to our country.

Chapter Twenty-Three

If Only They Knew

If only these Africans knew what people were paying for oceanfront property in a warm climate! If only they knew the millions of dollars these tourists would bring into their country. If only they knew the jobs it would create. If only they knew how valuable this resource was that was being destroyed.

We stopped for a moment along the beach. I got out of our vehicle and gazed out into the ocean. I closed my eyes and felt the warm sun and gentle breezes. I heard the waves as they crashed upon shore. It was so easy to imagine myself being at a beautiful vacation resort. As I kept my eyes closed, I wondered what people would pay to be in a place like this.

And then I opened my eyes, and the dream immediately vanished. I had seen very few bathrooms, but I knew there had to be some. Two rather large trucks with tanks on them were backed up to the ocean and were dumping raw sewage directly into the ocean.

The weather was very hot, and the ocean breezes did make it feel cooler. That is probably why many shepherds had their animals at the beach. There were goats, sheep, and some odd-looking cattle. I am not sure if it was the cattle or the sewage that created the unique smell.

We had strict instructions not to drink any water unless it was in sealed containers, and I was beginning to understand why. It seemed as if people were content living this way. If only I could help them see how to take care of this valuable oceanfront.

And then a thought came to me: Who was I to think that I was so smart and that I could teach them anything? I came from a very advanced country that has waste treatment plants and recycling programs. Yet a city less than three hours from where I live, Milwaukee, regularly dumps sewage into Lake Michigan.

If nothing else, I have a greater appreciation for our natural resources. At times, it seems the laws protecting them seem like overkill. But I truly wish that the generations after me would have water like that of the mountains in Yellowstone and not like that of the beaches I saw in Africa.

--------- *Chapter Twenty-Four* ---------

Radio

During our stay in Africa, we had little idea what was going on in the rest of the world. I think I saw two or three television sets. They were in the city, where people would go to sell their goods. It was easy to tell when there was a TV around, because people were crowded all around it. These television sets were not showing any news or even any current shows. We saw mostly very old American TV shows being played.

Some of the reason for very limited television was because of poverty, but it seems that was not the main reason. The government did not want to give information to the people. They were hoping that would keep them from rebellion. Most people in Africa have no idea what it is like in America—or any other country for that matter.

We can access instant information from all over the world, and we have many resources with which to do it. We have newspapers and magazines delivered right to our doors. We have twenty-four-hour news channels and Internet access to millions of pieces of information.

One of our main missions on our trip to Africa was to investigate building a radio station there. Radio is extremely important to the Africans; it is their only real connection to the outside world. Radios are also quite inexpensive, so many can own them.

The government is very cautious about what is said on their radio waves. They do not want anyone to inform the people and rally them to overthrow the wicked government.

Lack of knowledge is huge problem in Africa, and it seems it is very hard to change that. If we give them fish, we feed them for a day; if we teach them to fish, we feed them for a lifetime. Breaking through the barriers to teach them to fish was much harder than I expected.

—————— *Chapter Twenty-Five* ——————

Garbage Everywhere

I realize that you may not be surprised to hear that in Africa, there is garbage everywhere. And maybe I also expected to see that even before going there. So then what is the lesson behind the sight of garbage everywhere?

I have been to Disney World a number of times. It is extremely impressive to see all the creativity and the ideas that have been brought to life. Disney seems to have a way of wowing us with their creativity and their ability to deliver memories and fun.

But what about their garbage? Have you been wowed by their garbage—or, shall I say, their lack of garbage? I must admit that I was continually impressed with the effort they put into keeping things clean. People were constantly sweeping and cleaning everywhere.

Do you think that it was important for them to have things clean and orderly? What does that immediately say about the leadership behind Disney?

While traveling through the bush, we stopped for a moment to rest. One of our guys noticed an empty juice carton that had fallen out of our van. He picked it up and put it back in the van. Upon returning to the van, he again noticed that it was on the ground and once again picked it up. Our host took it from him and threw it back on the ground. "Where else are you going to put it?" he asked.

My father-in-law, Norman, always told me that you could tell a lot about a person by what they leave lying around. He said you could drive down the road and instantly tell what kind of person lived there just by looking at how things are cared for. And it appears this lesson also applies to businesses, cities, and even countries.

Next time, before you think about throwing some garbage out the window, ask yourself this question: *If everyone in this country cared for it like me, would it be more like Africa or Disney?* And why not go another step and pick up someone else's garbage as you walk across the parking lot?

With all due respect to the people of Africa, they don't have dumpsters and regularly scheduled garbage pickup. They don't have money for food, much less the resources to deal with garbage. I am thankful that I was born in America, and I am willing to do my part to have it look more like Disney World.

Chapter Twenty-Six

For Sale: Stump

Our two children have heard this story many times since my return from Africa. It seems that every time they complain about the responsibilities they have, I feel compelled to tell them this story.

We were driving down the road out in the middle of nowhere. It was many miles to the nearest town. The temperature was in the mid-nineties. And just in case you forgot, the roads were more like wide deer trails.

We were always very alert while driving, not only so we wouldn't fall into a huge pothole, but also because every mile seemed to have something unusual. We could see something off in the distance; it was in the middle of the road and was not moving. As we got closer, we could see that it was a small boy.

He was maybe seven or eight years old. He had a wagon behind him that had on it a very large stump. The wagons were quite common. They looked as if they were made from old car axles; they even had full-size car tires on all four wheels. This was a wagon big enough that we would all use a tractor or some vehicle to pull it. The wagon alone must have been very heavy, even without the large tree stump on it. This small boy was in the process of taking this stump to town to sell. The nearest town was still many miles away, and who knew how far he had already traveled.

Most of the cooking there was done with coal or wood. The African people did not have electricity and therefore no ovens or microwaves. Those who could not afford coal would try to find wood to cook with. Trees there were very limited, so even wood was a rare commodity. This stump would hold absolutely no value in America, but for this little boy, it might allow him to barter for food to help feed his family.

It was not uncommon to have children entering the workforce at five or six years old. And they were not working to buy gas for their cars or to get the latest video game. They were working for survival. They were often working for their next meal.

If only our youth in America today could live just one hour of that little boy's life. Young people in this country are so blessed. Don't get me wrong—that can be a good thing. I just wish they knew how blessed they really are.

Chapter Twenty-Seven

Halftime

Yes, it is true: we are halfway through our journey through this book. I think that it is time to take a break. I think it may be time to answer a few of the questions I have received. It is also time to reflect on the motives and to measure the fruit.

It seems like only yesterday that the scales were removed from my eyes. It was as if I was able for the first time to see. The bubble that contained my life had exploded. For the first time, I saw what life is like for millions of people less fortunate than I. It did not take long for me to realize that my life would never be the same.

People regularly ask, "Why did you go?" It is an important question that deserves an answer. It is, however, a question that cannot be fully answered here because of my promise to keep these short.

But I will tell you this. I was talking one day to a person who has been very influential in my life. I was sharing with him the passion or fire burning within me to have a positive influence in the lives of others. He went on to tell me that most all people who have left a great legacy were jump-started by one thing.

That one thing was to do something bigger than themselves. He went on to define it as doing something almost impossible. It needed to be something that other people would call you crazy for doing, and it needed to done for others. Out of that discussion, my mission to Africa was born.

"Why did you write about your lessons or experiences?" some people ask. "There must be a catch. People just don't do things like this without expecting something."

Okay, okay ... I am expecting something, and I am expecting it from you. I am hoping to pass on some of what I saw and much of what I learned. Why?

Because I hope that you too will become more thankful for all that you have: more thankful for the people around you; more thankful for the country that you live in and for the people who have fought and are still fighting for it; more thankful for your possessions and yet at the same time less driven by them; and so on. Thankfulness brings many things, including joy. And like many negative things, thankfulness is contagious.

My hope is to somehow give to you some of what Africa has given to me. But why? So that you too will realize that life is not all about us. So that you too will realize true joy and happiness is measured not by what we own, but by what we give.

My hope is to get you to understand how blessed you really are. My hope is to inspire you to use what has been placed on the inside of you to help make a difference. Make a difference in your family, your business, your community, and our world. One person can change the world, and that person could be you.

Chapter Twenty-Eight

No Guns and No Revolution

Two weeks ago, someone asked me if people were still being taken as slaves. Even though I have spent ten days in Africa, I am by no means an expert. But to my knowledge, millions of people are no longer being captured like animals, stripped from their families, and sent to foreign lands never to be seen again. That does not mean that slavery is no longer happening in Africa or in other countries. It may even be a version of slavery worse than having a family member stolen from you.

In many parts of Africa, people are not allowed to have guns or weapons. The main motive behind this is to keep the people from continual revolution. Yes, the governments are often corrupt and wicked. And that in itself would invite revolution without even taking into consideration the poverty in which the people live.

The governments themselves are also very weak and lack any real way of defending themselves. Because of this, Africa is a hotbed for terrorist groups to set up camp. The governments are easily overthrown, and the people have no weapons to defend themselves.

They cannot call 911. They cannot call the police. They cannot call anyone. They have no phones, no two-way radios, and not even a vehicle to use to escape this atrocity. This type of slavery may be even worse; the people are completely at the mercy of these ruthless terrorists. Close your eyes and imagine you and your family in that position.

The extreme poverty and lack of opportunity has been enslaved in their lifestyle. There are no manufacturing plants to work in. You cannot just spend the day putting in applications for work in Africa. In America, even a homeless person could quite easily get a job and go from rags to riches.

America is truly a land of opportunity. This land truly is the home of the brave. And like never before, I realize it is also a land of freedom. We have rights in this country that really should be seen as privileges. They came at a cost and are not universal all over the world.

You and your family are very blessed to call this country your home.

————— *Chapter Twenty-Nine* —————

Bang

Today we are committing some time to do some shopping! We are halfway through our stay in Africa, and it is time to start to think about what to bring home.

Many people come from the bush into the city to sell their goods. There are no Walmarts or Farm and Fleets to visit. No air-conditioned malls to spend the day shopping in. This is a city of over 750,000 people, and it is like the biggest flea market you will ever see. The streets, better described as dirt trails, are lined on both sides with little stands selling everything you can imagine. There will be a future lesson that tells more about sales technique in Africa.

We had been to this same city and same part of town after dark. Many of the shops were shut down. Many of the goods were left as is. Some were covered with blankets because of all the dust. But they were left unattended in remote parts of town, where they could be easily stolen.

This is a place of extreme poverty; people were starving. Yet things were not being stolen. How could this be? There were few buildings, and most did not have doors or locks of any kind. Gold was quite common, and even that seemed to lack the protection that I would expect.

I asked our host if there was any problem with stealing. He replied that stealing, at least in this part of Africa, was extremely rare. He could see by the look on my face that I could not understand how that could be.

He then pointed toward a man dressed in camouflage and armed with a machine gun. He proceeded to tell me that if this man sees anyone steal, he doesn't capture and arrest the person. He doesn't read him his rights or carefully go through all of the steps required so that the case will not be thrown out of court later. He does not take him to jail or even fine him for what he has stolen.

He simply points his gun and BANG! The thief is shot, with no questions asked. And as if that is not bad enough, the body is not removed. The family of the dead thief can come and remove the body. If not, it will remain as a testimony for others to see that stealing in Africa does not pay.

Chapter Thirty

Don't Worry, Be Happy

As I pointed out earlier, the people of Africa have a very high level of love and compassion. It is very easily seen in their faces and in all that they say and do. They were a living example for me to remember. Their level of love and compassion was like snow in Mexico: it just seemed like it couldn't be there. How could people who have so little, love so much?

Even though I had a very high level of respect for the love they showed to us, and to each other, something was missing. Looking into their eyes or watching them communicate left me feeling empty or sad. And I was quite sure that it was not coming from their very evident poverty. The sadness that I was feeling did not come because they were without food, clothing, or housing.

Finally, after some real soul-searching I realized what I believe was the missing ingredient: there was no joy and laughter. It dawned on me that I had not seen any joy and laughter in their expressions or their words.

That realization came through Kevin, one of the guys who came with us on the trip. He is a very big man who seems to always be full of joy and laughter, regardless of the circumstances around him. People were always looking at him very strangely in Africa (and back in America also). I realize he was very big and very white, and just from that perspective alone, he really stuck out!

But I believe it was his huge, unending joy and laughter that these people had never seen before. They looked at him almost as if he wasn't real or as if he had some kind of disease. They couldn't attribute it to drunkenness, because they don't have money to waste on that over there—and besides that, Kevin doesn't drink.

Why couldn't they be happy? Why couldn't they laugh? Why couldn't they show some expression of joy and happiness? Was it the poverty they lived in that prevented them from joy? Could it be the feeling of imprisonment or the lack of options available to them to alter their lives? Could it be all the lessons and experiences of abuse and hardship passed down from generation to generation? Could it be worry or lack of hope that kept them from discovering the hidden treasure inside of joy and happiness?

My answer to all those questions is that I don't know. But this I do know: I am now more thankful for people like Kevin, who always seem to bring smiles and laughter regardless of what is going on around them. I now place a much higher price or value on joy and happiness. Love and compassion are extremely important, but without joy and happiness, they seem empty.

This week, recognize and thank the Kevins in your life. If you don't have any, find some, because your life is missing something.

Chapter Thirty-One

Job Opening

The next day, our travel once again got us out into the bush. And like every day so far, the day offered something unusual to see and learn. We were on a road that appears to be having some work done on it. Remember that our trails in our national forests are like highways compared to the roads in Africa. And hopefully after this chapter's lesson, you will better understand why.

As we moved slowly down the so-called road, I saw a truck off to our right. Like most vehicles, it was very, very old. No new vehicles ever make it to Africa. Many of our very old, oil-burning, and obsolete vehicles end up in Africa. And here was one of them, parked about seventy-five yards off the road.

It wasn't the truck that kept my attention, but was what was happening with it. It was being loaded with gravel—not gravel that had been run through a crusher and was processed to just the right size, but stones of all sizes mixed with dirt that closely resembled clay. Because of the soil type and lack of rain, this dirt was very, very hard.

The fact that a truck was being loaded with this may not seem all that unusual, but the stones and dirt were being dug from the ground by hand—not with shovels, picks, or other tools, but by hand. And those hands did not have nice leather gloves to protect them.

This gravel was not only being dug by hand, but was also being loaded that way. The workers were carrying the baskets of stone and dirt mined with their bare hands on their heads to the truck. They had built ramps on each side of the truck with the dirt they had mined and carried there. And then about twenty people on each side of the truck were carrying baskets filled with dirt and stone, dumping them onto the truck.

How much would you have to be paid to do this for an entire day in ninety-five-degree heat? Many of these people were women who also had to find some way to survive. Some of the best jobs paid up to two dollars per day! This job likely paid much less. And for those of you business-minded individuals who think that the cost of living must also be much lower, a loaf of bread costs a dollar! Yes, a half-day of work for a loaf of bread!

Please take a moment, close your eyes, and realize that this is happening right now, as you read this, in many places throughout our world. I don't care how bad you may think your job is, be thankful for it; your worst day will not likely come close to even the best workday in Africa. And please, if you understand this but know someone else who doesn't, teach them. If that doesn't work, send them to me—or better yet, buy them a plane ticket to Africa.

---------------- *Chapter Thirty-Two* ----------------

How Can I Get to America?

On one day during our trip, Kevin and I had a chance to spend some time on the streets of the city. We felt that we had been there long enough that we could venture out a little on our own. I felt quite nervous walking down these streets; not only was everybody different, but they all seemed to be looking at us.

It was almost as if we had arrived in a time machine after having gone back at least a hundred years. People would just stop what they were doing and stare as we walked by. I wondered what was going through their minds.

We came across many children and teenagers who were trying to sell things. They were serious and determined to sell what they had. Never did I see any purple hair, tattoos, or earrings in places they shouldn't be. These young people were not trying to draw any attention to themselves; they were instead focused on survival.

One young man came up to us with a mission: He wanted to know about America. He had heard some stories and wanted to know if they were true. He talked about how he had heard about this magnificent kingdom called America. He talked about it as if it was a magnificent story or fairy tale, something too good to be true.

We assured him that those things were indeed true, and that America was real. His eyes got wide, and he seemed to hang on every word as we expanded his thinking by telling him more about our homes, our businesses, and our wonderful country. He listened with great interest, and then something happened that made me wish I had never met him.

He asked a question that was followed by many more, only said in a different way. "How can I get to America?" he asked with every ounce of sincerity and determination that he had. "Please take me with you?" he begged. "I will wash and shine your car every day. I will work for you for free—please, please, take me with you to America."

We tried to convince him that it was not possible, but he would not give up. We were forced to leave, with him clinging to us, still trying to convince us to somehow take him along, to that magical place he had heard of, called America.

---------------- *Chapter Thirty-Three* ----------------

I'm Bored

I am sure that if you are a parent, you have heard your children complain of boredom a thousand times. It seems that as I talk to people older than I am, or read books authored by people much older than I am, I realize that a transformation has taken place. Our children have so much more to do than any generation before us, yet seem to be bored or less fulfilled than others who have so much less.

Actually, my observation while in Africa went much deeper than that. It seems that this transformation may have started in the previous generation, because it is even very visible in many adults in our country. The reason I am assuming that this has not always been the case is because of history books and lessons. Stories about the Pilgrims and the settlers who pushed our country west seem to give no evidence of this attitude or type of culture.

We as Americans spend millions and millions of dollars every day on entertainment. You may think that this is normal or just a part of life. I can assure you that much of the rest of the world does not share this pleasure.

Next time you go to Circuit City or Best Buy, ask yourself what in that store is a necessity and what is purely entertainment.

There will be no extravagant sound systems or car stereos in Africa. No VCRs, DVDs, or computer software. No video games or electronic toys of any kind.

They don't have boats, ATVs, and snowmobiles. They don't have movie theaters or sports bars lined with televisions. They don't have stock-car races or demolition derbies. They don't have carnivals or theme parks.

They don't pay people millions of dollars to play a game, just so they can watch them. Think about the place we give professional sports in our lives. You would think that our very lives depended on sports.

Am I being too harsh on our people? Depends. Our country is a beautiful place, but there are some trends that point to trouble in the future. If you have trouble accepting or even seeing what I am talking about, please, go to a place like Africa and look from the outside facing in. We are a country that seems to be addicted to entertainment. Listen to people as they talk. How often does the conversation surround singers, actors, professional athletes, TV shows, or other things connected to entertainment?

Evaluate your life this week and try to realize how much of it is filled with entertainment. Entertainment is not all bad, but if too much of our lives are filled with it, we can't possibly have the time or energy to grow ourselves or others. You, your children, your friends and family, and every other human being are born with tremendous gifts and talents—talents that must be grown, developed, and shared. Don't allow too much entertainment to force you to take those precious gifts to the grave with you.

---------------- *Chapter Thirty-Four* ----------------

What Is Wrong with My Heart?

I didn't know if I could take this anymore. We were three-fourths of our way through our time in Africa. The problem was not the absence of Pam, even though I missed her tremendously, or that I had not been able to call or speak to anyone back home. I did wonder daily how my children were, and if everything was OK, but my anxiety, sadness, frustration, and overwhelming feeling of emptiness seems to be coming from somewhere else.

I had not found any food that even came close to Pam's roast with mashed potatoes and gravy, but that was not the problem. I didn't think the very limited sleep or the long days were the foundation of this inner frustration either.

Could it be the fact that we had no idea what was going on anywhere else in the world? I didn't think so. In Africa, there is no way to know what is happening anywhere, even locally. When it comes to news, what you see with your eyes is what you get—no CNN or local TV station to tune into. No Internet to surf in order to quickly become informed of what is going on at that very second around the world. No magazine or newspaper of any kind.

So what was it? What was this frustration that seemed to be building daily coming from? Being totally, and I mean totally, isolated from everything else my life had touched to that point, was at times scary and almost overwhelming. But it was also that total separation from everything that forced me to think about things I had never thought of before. Maybe this had something to do with why I was encouraged to do something bigger than myself.

The purpose of our mission to Africa had been clearly established before we left. It was to give of ourselves, to people who had less than us, halfway around the world. It was a grand vision, maybe a start of something that could possibly change a nation or an entire continent. Much of this frustration—perhaps better described as inner pain—was coming from this purpose not being fulfilled.

We were there to help. We were there to make a difference. The idea was to teach them to fish, not to just give them fish to eat for a day. Yet every second I was with them, I felt like Santa Claus. People were always looking at my hand. They would just stare at my hand. And if I would take out some money and give it to them, they would quickly put it away and ask for more.

Why? Could it be because they thought what was in my hand was more valuable than what was in my heart? I believe it was because they did not understand that who a person is on the inside is much more important, and far more valuable, than what they have on the outside. I understand that they have nothing, and many are forced to watch their children die of starvation right before their eyes—what a horrible thing to experience. I am sure that all of us would seek help anywhere we could, and we might behave the same way if we were in their position.

But what about countries like ours—places of true abundance? Are we content with what we have? Are we seeing what is truly valuable inside of us and others? Are we thankful for even the small things around us, or are we always looking for more? Everywhere we drive, there are more storage sheds being built to store our things—could that be a clue? I am guilty, but after my trip to Africa I will never again place more value on what a person owns or has. I will never forget that it is what is on the inside that really counts!

Chapter Thirty-Five

Giant Toothpicks

We had been in Africa for over a week now, and there had not been a day that I had not seen a person walking around with what appeared to be a tree in their mouth. Africa is a place that doesn't have high standards for eating habits, without much emphasis placed on things like having the right silverware or proper table manners. These people are focused on survival.

I began to wonder, though, about their teeth. Their teeth are beautiful, incredibly white, and extremely healthy. People in America pay large sums of money to have teeth like these. What was their secret? Could it have something to do with that tree in their mouth?

People of all ages, from very young to very old, had them. Both men and women carried the giant toothpicks between their teeth. These toothpicks all were unprocessed and varied greatly in size. They were like branches broken off of trees and cut to somewhere between two and six inches long. Most were no smaller than the diameter of a pencil.

Why were they using them? Was it a tradition or some kind of ritual that signified something? I had found that the best way to get a question answered was to ask it. "Why were they using those trees in their mouths?" I asked.

Our guide had that puzzled look on his face that made me feel as if I had just asked a really dumb question. Could it be possible that I did not know about quinine? After realizing that I indeed had never heard of quinine, he proceeded to tell me about the miracle tree.

Quinine is a substance found in a tree, and it possesses many natural healing qualities. Africans use it for their teeth to prevent any buildup or gum disease. They use the square end of the giant toothpick to brush and clean their teeth, then keep it in their mouths to draw out the juices from the tree.

Quinine has a bitter taste but is a very inexpensive solution to a continent without dentists, doctors, or hospitals. Quinine is also used against malaria, heart problems, and many other physical problems. Does it work? I have never seen teeth like those in Africa. They are strong, straight, and shiny like ivory.

Of course, Africans realize that if they lose their teeth, there are no options—no root canals, caps, crowns, or false teeth. They also do not have all of the kitchen tools we have to process their food.

In America, we use cigarettes to make our teeth brown and to slowly kill ourselves. In Africa, they use giant, bitter–tasting toothpicks to save their teeth and extend their lives.

─────────── *Chapter Thirty-Six* ───────────

The Value of Relationships

Since my trip to Africa, I have found many, many, things to be thankful for. There have also been some things that I miss or things that I wish could be different here in America.

Don't get me wrong—I am very thankful for our country. Very often, there are benefits to American life that we cannot see until we step away from where we live. We somehow get lulled into thinking that people in the rest of the world are just like us. They are not, and this chapter's lesson is about something that is becoming less and less common in our culture here in America.

It is not that the people of Africa have figured out the value of relationships and fought against anything that would come against them. I don't think it is that they realize how important relationships are and automatically teach this philosophy to their children as something never to be lost.

That respect for relationships is there, but I believe it is by default. The people that I saw in Africa were always together. Everywhere I went, people would be walking together—not because they were exercising or just valued the time with each other, but because that is their form of transportation. It often takes hours or even days to get to your destination, with no radio to listen to and no comfortable seat to recline in while the other person drives.

I love to learn, and while in one of the most poverty-stricken countries in the world, I did just that. My time in Africa has changed my life forever; the people there have taught me so much, even though they have so little. No, our family has not taken up walking as our main form of transportation. But many other things have changed. Often, if there is more than one of us in the car, the radio is off-limits. We try not to let the radio or anything else rob us of something very valuable called relationships. Our daughter Laura loves music and just received an iPod for her birthday. She quickly learned that it would not be used while in the car—or at any other time when a person important to her is nearby.

Our young people and adults can always be seen with some sort of music in their ears, even when they are together as a group. Drive past any high school or college campus, and you will see students with cords in their ears that look like walking zombies. They are walking together, but they are not talking, laughing, or enjoying each other's presence.

I don't have the space to fully express how I think we in America are making a big mistake by slowly losing this very important activity of relating to one another. We are so busy chasing things, and many of us have a disease that I have heard called "the desire to acquire." We want the newest and latest technology—and will use borrowed money to get it. After my trip to Africa, it became very clear to me that technology is one of the biggest enemies to relationships. It is often not the invention itself, or even the use of it, but our frenzy to work to pay for all of it that suffocates the relationships around us.

I grew up on a farm and always had the opportunity to eat dinner with my family. I realize now that I had taken it for granted. Our family now does more camping and other things that are built more on the value of relationships, rather than pleasure. We play games, take walks or bike rides, or just sit around and talk.

In conversations with my elders, it seems that the generations before us, like the people in Africa, regularly spent time with others.

Could it be that the current condition of our economy, with all the credit card debt, bankruptcies, and fiscal horror stories, is telling us something? Someone once verbalized to me a valuable lesson that really applies here: "Never let the things that matter most be at the mercy of things that matter least." Before going to the next chapter, take some time as an individual, and as a family, to really think about what belongs on the list of things that matter most. The steps that you take to protect the things that matter most will greatly influence the rest of your life—and the lives of those after you.

―――――――― *Chapter Thirty-Seven* ――――――――

Family Values

In Africa, it is not uncommon to see children living like wild animals. Their parents have perished, and there is no one to care for them. They have no home to go to—no shelter or government program to support them.

They will roam about, digging through garbage in an attempt to survive. And the garbage in a place where people are starving is much different than the garbage outside of most, if not all, eating places here in America. In many places in Africa, it has become a real problem, because groups of homeless children are attacking others to steal from them—not for fun or because of their wants, but to live another day. In many large cities, there can be hundreds or even thousands of children like this.

Wishing to learn and understand all I could during this life-changing season, I asked another question that would alter my daily thoughts forever: "Why are these people having all these children if they are not sure they can care for them? How can anyone have a child knowing that the child will likely starve to death?"

The answer astonished me: Many of these African parents will have twenty or more children, and it is not because of the lack of birth control. They have as many children as possible in hope that one of them will survive and be able to care for them! They have no nursing homes or any kind of elderly care—no Social Security, government programs, or insurance to depend on after they are unable to work.

As my heart locked on to every child I saw during the rest of my stay in Africa, a small rage grew in me toward the parents who chose to have all those children. How could they do this? Wasn't it selfish to have all these children just so that maybe one would make it and be able to care for them when they were old? At least in our highly advanced country of America, this did not happen, I thought. Or did it?

Then it occurred to me that I should reserve judgment on these people in Africa because in America, we don't have thousands of homeless children wandering the streets, because we think nothing of killing them before they are born. Are we not just as selfish here in America? At least in Africa, the choice is based on survival.

Then there are the current and all-too-common discussions of same-sex marriages all across our country. In Africa, people are still stoned for such crazy and—in my opinion—immoral behavior.

I also just learned the other day that in a hospital less than an hour from my home, we have a world-famous doctor who is paid a huge amount of money. In fact, an entire floor at that hospital is devoted to his work. And if you have a few hundred thousand dollars to spend, and you don't like being a man, he can change you into a woman!

At least the decisions in Africa are based on life and death. Here in America, I am embarrassed to say, we spend millions and millions of dollars that could be used to feed the world on our own selfish desires. We are spoiled brats instead of people who are a solution to the rest of the world. Do you think that this is too harsh? Please look at the balance sheets of our people, our businesses, and our country before you decide. And worse yet, look at what all of the money was spent on.

──────── *Chapter Thirty-Eight* ────────

Make a Difference

I must admit that there were days when I wished that I could have snapped my fingers and been back home. And then hardly a minute passed by, and another experience robbed me of the pleasure of thinking of home.

We would return to our beds at night, totally exhausted by the day's sights and experiences. We would rise thinking that yesterday must have been a dream. We would open our suitcases and look at our American possessions and momentarily think that this place we visited yesterday was not real.

I catch my mind trying to convince me that it was not possible to have a place like this on the same earth with America. Just seven days before, I had been in a place that had everything imaginable. I was in a home fit for a king. I could go on the Internet and buy anything and even have it shipped to my home.

I was safe and protected. I had little fear of my family being captured or killed. I had the freedom to go where I wanted, when I wanted. I had stability and a future. I knew that my children could attend school and continue beyond that with unlimited choices for education. I knew that any person had many opportunities to work and to provide for their families.

How could this place called Africa be different? My mind was trying to tell my eyes that what they were seeing was not true. I guess I thought that somehow every country had what we have in America. Every morning, I would find myself in this mental battle: Was yesterday a dream? Can heaven and hell exist on the same planet?

And then it would happen: I would close my suitcase and put away the pictures of my wife and my children. I would open the door and leave that place where I had slept for the night—a place where, in the dark, I was free to think and believe anything I wanted.

And then, just like the day before, my mind could no longer argue with what my eyes could see. For those of you who will never have the opportunity to visit a place like Africa, please, listen to me. Be thankful for all that you have. Be careful that your drive for more does not cloud your ability to see and be truly grateful for what you already have. Live every day with love, joy, and purpose. Why were you and I born in America instead of Africa? Was it an accident, or is there a reason?

This I do know: I am thankful and I will do my part to make a difference. I will do my best to develop and use the gifts given to me to help others. I will do what I can to inspire others and encourage them to use the greatness placed inside of them. You may never go to Africa or have any desire to make a difference in the lives of people in a Third World country. What about friends, family, co-workers, neighbors, or that person on the bus that you will never see again? We need you to help make this world a better place, even if it is in the small portion of it you that you call yours.

Chapter Thirty-Nine

The Art of Selling

The next two chapters will address some sales techniques from Africa. Some are good, and I think that even our best salespeople would have been impressed. And some are downright disgusting.

I did not see any Walmart Superstores during my stay. I saw no local grocery or department stores to run and get what you needed. Pam would not like the shopping opportunities in Togo, Africa!

It is not that people did not have needs. The people of Togo still needed to eat and purchase some basic things. But the economy could not support such buildings. I admit I was irritated, and yet at the same time impressed, with how buyers and sellers often met.

Many, many items that are outdated or deemed useless in other countries are shipped to places like Africa. It seems we are always willing to give away what has little value, and America is no different. I saw many things from America being sold that could not be given away back home—things like old music from long before my time. It is amazing that anything that somehow was connected to America had value to them.

There are not abundant jobs to support the rather large families—or, in other words, there are many more people looking to sell goods than there are people who have the ability to buy them. I guess you could say that the same is true in America; it is only what is being sold that is different.

In America, when things are bought and sold, the bottom line of the business is at stake. In Africa, it is the very life of that person or their family that is at stake. Talk about motivation to sell! People are lined up at every intersection; they will be in lines eight or ten people deep. As cars stop at each intersection, people will swarm every car trying to sell their product.

They will tap on every window and show you what they have, strongly persuading you to buy it.

They had everything you could imagine on their heads and ready for immediate sale—everything from food (which we were advised not to eat) to some of the most unusual things I have ever seen in my life. Because of the life-or-death system of survival connected to their sales success, I can assure you these people were determined to sell.

Chapter forty will have a look at a rather disgusting sales department.

Chapter Forty

The Art of Selling—Part II

On our ninth day in Africa, we began our trip back to the airport in Accra, on our way back home. Like every other day in Africa so far, it would be one filled with challenge and opportunity. But before I describe that day, I want to finish describing the art of selling in Africa. This chapter addresses two rather disgusting products for sale.

The first one I will mention may not be all that unusual for the person trying to sell it, or the person who would like to buy it. We saw three or four of these on our way back to the airport.

The seller is standing out by the road, holding up his product until a buyer happens to come by to purchase or trade for it. Remember the temperature is in the nineties, and most homes do not have refrigerators. I am not sure how long this person has been out in this heat with his merchandise, and we did not want to stop and find out.

What was for sale was being held by its long tail and looked as if it belonged on Survivor or Fear Factor. It was the biggest rat I had ever seen! Including the tail, these rats were eighteen to twenty-four inches long. I was thankful that I not only did not have to eat one, but also that I did not have to live with them.

The second thing that I saw for sale in Africa brought feelings of disgust, anger, and embarrassment. It was not just the product in this case that disgusted me, but even more the purchasers of them. If there is one thing that really irritates me, it is when people take advantage of other people, especially when people who have much take advantage of others who have so little.

The French at one time ruled the area where we stayed in Africa. Therefore, not only is French the most common language, but the French also are the most common visitors to this country. This chapter may also give another clue why the welcome mat is not thrown out to visitors.

I saw far too many French-speaking men in their forties and fifties who seemed to be coming for this second product. Why would they take advantage of people like this? What they are doing is wrong in any country, but taking advantage of people who would sell anything to survive seems so much worse. The poor who are forced to sell themselves to survive may suffer now, but the rich who take advantage of them will get their turn.

—————— *Chapter Forty-One* ——————

Trouble or Opportunity?

I mentioned in the last chapter that we were beginning our journey back to the airport. It seemed as if we had been there a lifetime. And even though this ten-day experience had altered my life forever, it felt as if I was leaving with more questions than answers. It still seemed as if I was in a dream, and that this was not real.

The next step of our journey toward home was to get to the airport. It proved to be no small challenge. It would require a day's travel back through some of the same checkpoints we had passed through on our way here. I was still in awe—or maybe better described as still in shock—at what I had seen every day so far. I no longer had any preconceived notions of what to expect each morning before a new day began.

I had resigned myself to just take every day and do my best with what it delivered. It was impossible to deny any longer that this was real. This was not a vacation by any means. Yet, somehow deep inside, I knew that somewhere this trip possessed great treasure. I promised to both learn all I could and give all that I could.

It was a lesson that was valuable then and maybe even more valuable now. Every day is a chance to start over. Every day is a chance to be sad or happy. Every day is a chance to be thankful or ungrateful. Every day is a chance to complain about what this life has given us or a chance to birth what this life can become. It is a chance to focus on our troubles or problems or a chance to discover the day's opportunities.

This day, like all of the rest before it, would be a day to make a choice: thankfulness, faith, and perseverance, or fear and worry.

Our van, which had well over two hundred thousand miles on its odometer, did not seem very happy about the journey. We had barely made it to the first small town, and the engine was overheating. Even though the temperatures were in the nineties, it was not a journey through a tropical paradise. We would need to travel many miles through a dry and barren land that seemed to be unable to support any life.

We were able to scare up some water for our radiator, so we could continue. But just when we thought our troubles for the day were over, the van once again forced us to stop. What was this village like? Would they welcome us? What would their feelings be toward two white guys? Would this village present trouble or opportunity?

Chapter Forty-Two

Friend or Enemy?

There we were, sitting in a van in the middle of Africa. I had felt quite safe while our escort was with us. He had left us to look for more water for our van or some other solution to our transportation problem.

Kevin and I scanned the area, and it seemed as if people were not moving. It was almost as if a parade were going through their village. Why were they all looking at us? Why were they staring and pointing? Were they friends or enemies? Could they speak English?

As Kevin and I pondered these and many more questions, only one answer seemed to come up: the only way we would ever know the answers to those questions was to go and find out. We slowly stepped out of the van almost as if we expected something to happen. It was as if life was once again in slow motion.

We had left the comfort of our escort and our van. We were in a place that the rest of the world probably didn't even know existed. No person ever came here to shop, vacation, or look for a job. It began to dawn on me why we looked so out of place: many of those people probably never saw people as white as us. And I found out in a hurry that they were as concerned about us as we were about them.

We walked less than one hundred feet before attempting to talk to someone. Two ladies were sewing outside what was likely their home. It was a building about eight feet wide and ten feet long; like many of the homes I had seen, it had a dirt floor and possessed none of the other conveniences we in America think come standard with every home.

They were using a sewing machine that required them to use one hand to turn a pulley on one end of the machine while feeding the thread and cloth in with the other. They were quite skilled, even though they were using primitive equipment. We asked a couple questions and came to the conclusion that they could not speak English.

Then, out of the corner of my eye, I noticed a few men off to our right. They were slowly coming closer and had very concerned looks on their faces. Immediately, I realized these people could have had grandparents who were captured as slaves. These people had every right to be very concerned about us!

You already know that we came back alive, but you will need to wait until next chapter to find out if we found friends or enemies in this village.

—————— *Chapter Forty-Three* ——————

Smile, Shake, and Hug

The choices that we make really do have a very large impact on the outcome of our lives. And I must admit that at this moment, I was beginning to question our choice to leave the protection of our vehicle. Should we run, or should we try to communicate with these men and let them know that we mean no harm?

The incredible experience I gained from being involved in PDPW (Professional Dairy Producers of Wisconsin) really helped here. I had been taught to be proactive instead of reactive. The right option was to talk with them ... but how? I immediately found myself recalling the media training class that I had also taken during my time at PDPW.

We put smiles on our faces, stretched out our hands to signal friendship, and moved toward them. Almost immediately, the entire atmosphere changed. In the next few seconds of our lives, a magical thing happened. What we had thought was a bad situation was really quite the opposite. People who we thought were enemies were really just people that we perceived or judged improperly.

Yes, they were different from us—not just the color of their skin, but the way they lived and the food that they ate. But they were still people who had minds and hearts. They still had every reason to need friends more than they needed enemies.

These men could speak English, and we had an incredible experience with them. Like us, they realized that we were not enemies and meant no harm. How could our attitudes toward each other change so quickly? Why did we assume that they were not friends from the start?

I have thought about that experience many, many, times. How many times have I found myself in the same situation back here in America, wondering if people are friends or enemies? The lesson from that moment in time over a year ago on the continent of Africa is this: There are no enemies, only people we have been unable to turn into friends. It seems that my attitude toward others has a lot to do with whether I treat people around me as friends or enemies. Smile constantly, shake hands often, and hug regularly.

In the next chapter, you will learn more about our new friends and get to see the miracles these men were performing behind their house.

Chapter Forty-Four

Need or Want?

As we were escorted behind one man's home, I saw a number of very old vehicles. They were all at least twenty years old, and yes, it did look like a junkyard. It was easy to see that many of the vehicles had been sitting in that spot for many years. Remember, this was Africa—few people could afford to own a car, much less buy gas for one or maintain one.

There was no building other than the small shack they called home—no sign to indicate what they were doing with all these vehicles. I could not understand why this man was so excited. He was showing us all this as if he was a real-estate broker trying to sell us a new, state-of-the-art business.

He was obviously very proud of whatever they were doing. And once again, we found ourselves asking questions. "What is it that you are doing with these vehicles?" we asked. He took us around to the other side of a van we were standing by. I saw an older man, and one in his late teens or early twenties. They were both kneeling down next to this van.

As we approached, they stood and welcomed us. I will never forget what this young man was holding. In one hand he held a hammer. This was no ordinary hammer; the handle was broken and was now only six or seven inches long. In the other hand, he held a chisel. The chisel was very short—less than half its normal size. It was maybe four or five inches long, probably from being used for so long. These tools would never be used back home.

I still could not figure out what they were doing. The man then told us that they were restoring this van. Then the light bulb came on: this was a body shop! They all started to explain what they had done with this van. It was absolutely incredible.

They had replaced the entire side of this van. This may not sound like a big deal to you, but remember, they have no auto-parts stores; they cannot just order body parts and install them. They took old sheet metal and formed the entire side of this van with ... a very short chisel and a broken hammer!

We marveled at what they had done. It was incredible skill and craftsmanship. The people of Africa had just taught us another important lesson: Heart, soul, and determination are more important than the tools we own. Joy, thankfulness, and fulfillment do not come from possessions. The possessions that we think we need are really only wants.

In the next chapter, you will learn how these men and others became so skilled. Was it college, technical school, or an Internet course?

Chapter Forty-Five

Grow Yourself

I was beginning to feel very thankful that our van had broken down. If we had not had car troubles, we would have gone right through this village, and I would have missed some very important lessons. I wonder how many times I had gotten so tied up in my problems or circumstances, that I didn't see far enough ahead to realize the hidden treasure.

This was a village far different than the other places we had been. It was a long way from any city, and many of its residents probably never left this place their entire life. As we moved about, we not only saw the body shop, but also a place with a makeshift welder.

This guy was highly respected for his skill, even though he had no building in which to perform his trade. Even though I have taken many courses in welding and own a number of welders, I did not know that the pile of wires connected to a few small parts was a welder. Many of the wires were very brittle and had a number of bare spots on them.

We also saw an engine repair shop, complete with a homemade ramp to drive their vehicles up on to service them. I saw no hydraulic lifts or any other tools we expect to see at an auto-repair shop. And like all of the other businesses, this one had no buildings to cover the workers or protect them from the intense heat.

Anyone just driving through this village would have no idea all this was going on here. When we first arrived only hours ago, I viewed this small town as a junkyard that could not possibly hold any value. All the people we had met were amazingly proud and happy. And the skills they were performing were worth far more than the pennies they were happy to receive.

As I looked at the work they were doing, again with the same very primitive tools, I was again awestruck. How can these people do what they are doing? How did they learn these skills in this remote place? They obviously have no computers, no textbooks, and—in most cases—no schools.

Our host explained that when a person chooses the trade that he or she wants to enter, they seek a mentor. He or she is then required to work for that mentor a minimum of two years, often at a very low rate of pay, if any at all. This apprentice comes early and stays late and has deep respect for the knowledge being placed in him or her. When these apprentices have finished their tenures, they are free to try and find their own customers and one day become a mentor themselves.

Even in the remote places of Africa, I have seen the incredible value of growing yourself. Who is growing you? Who are you helping to grow?

Chapter Forty-Six

Balance

After I saw that this village was safe and the people seemed to welcome us, I went back to the van to get my camera. I was not about to let this very important moment in my life slip away without some pictures.

I decided to follow the same path we started with, beginning with the two ladies sewing. It was very easy to see that people were somewhat uncomfortable with what I was doing. Then I realized they probably had no idea what I was pointing at them.

I was using a digital camera and could therefore show them the picture that was taken. You would think that I had just flown in on some unusual flying spaceship. They could not understand how they could be inside of my camera. Before long we had a small crowd following us wanting their pictures taken. We have so much, and we take so much for granted.

After seeing what these people could accomplish with the little that they had, a lesson began to develop. The tools were primitive, yet the work was beautiful. They had never seen a camera or many of the material things we have back in America. Yet they seemed content, thankful, and even somewhat joyful.

Most of those people have no idea what we have in America. They do not get magazines or catalogs showing all the newest and greatest things. They do not get weekly sales bills showing all the newest styles of clothes. They are not bombarded with television commercials and billboards getting them to lust after things.

We have filters and auto parts delivered to our farm almost weekly. About once a month, the delivery person leaves a number of papers consisting of all the newest tools available and their sale prices. Our son usually points out the things that we need to have. A new tool for the people of Togo may be a broken one accidentally left in an old vehicle coming from another country.

I began to realize how our home and our lives are filled with this aggressive advertising. Newspapers and magazines are filled with advertisements showing us everything that would make our lives better and happier, if only we had them. We see what it is that they think will make us look good, feel good, or give us happiness and success. And we see it so often, and in so many places, that we start to believe it.

How much is enough? When should we be content with what we have? Since Africa, I have spent many hours teaching my children not to place things as a priority. At the end of the day it is not the things we own that bring joy. It is the relationships we have and the positive influences had on the life of others.

Over and over, we hear people at the end of their lives wish that they would have spent more of their life on relationships and less on the accumulation of things. It may once again not be intentional, but it looks like the poor people of Togo, Africa, may not be so poor after all. It is somewhat ironic—when we would pray for them, it would always contain heartfelt concern for their poverty. Almost every time I heard them pray for us or our country, it would include, "we pray that their abundance would not overtake them."

Chapter Forty-Seven

It's Not about Me

Our van had broken down *again*. The journey back to the airport seemed to be an entire adventure in itself. This time, we had stalled out in the bush, in the middle of nowhere. There was a building nearby; might someone live there?

Before we even got out of the van, a young lady came running to it. She spoke to our driver in a language we did not understand, then went running back to her home. In case you have forgotten, this home was not at all like any of the homes I have ever seen in America.

Before we knew it, she was on her way back toward us with two containers of water in her hands. She was also once again running. Here we are stranded out in the middle of Africa, and this lady was like an angel to us.

In less than an hour, we were once again on our way to the airport. I will never forget the kindness that lady showed us. If only I could have done something for her. I had left most of my clothes (from my suitcase) back in Togo. I had given away all of my money, except for enough to buy something to eat when we arrived in Amsterdam.

But I must admit that to this day I feel bad about not blessing that lady. What she did may not sound like much to you. But realize that water is not looked upon as something really valuable to us. They do not have electricity. They do not have wells or sewer systems. They cannot just go to a faucet and allow water to just flow from its spigot.

Much of their water comes from the nearest mud hole. After the rainy season, ponds of water are quite plentiful, but as the year goes on, they begin to dry up. They also get very dirty and contaminated. The same ponds are used for bathing, for washing clothes, and also by animals.

I had just come from a place where people were begging for money or things. They would always look at my hand instead of my face. This woman was making a tremendous sacrifice; she had given precious water, to people she didn't know, and expected nothing in return. If only I could have blessed her in some way.

Since that day, I have made a commitment to not only carry a fifty-dollar bill in a hidden place in my wallet, but to look for people like her. Those true servants are in every country and every city. I may never have the opportunity to bless that woman who gave her precious water to us, but I can assure you, her example was even more precious to me, and I promise to repeat it as many times as I can.

Chapter Forty-Eight

Airport at Last

We had finally made it back to the airport! It was mind-boggling to me to think about how much has happened in the last ten days. It was the same airport, yet it looked so much different than when we had first arrived. What once had appeared to be a run-down machine shed now looked so much nicer. Could they have improved it that much in the last nine days? Or could something have changed in how I was viewing it?

That return visit to the airport in Ghana was only the beginning of my reentry into the world. It seemed like thousands of thoughts and feelings were circling, fighting, trying to scramble for a place in my memory.

I was, and to be completely honest, still am, in a state of shock. All of the poverty and the corruption were almost unbearable to see. I was leaving Africa with feelings of thankfulness—not only for my country and all its blessings, but also for my life and all its relationships. I was leaving Africa with incredible thankfulness and respect for its people. They were required to endure what no person should need to experience. They had taught me so much.

I was also leaving Africa with feelings of resentment or anger toward anyone who was intentionally taking advantage of another.

Seeing the intense poverty left me sad and filled with compassion. But after finding out how the government confiscated everything of value, I will admit that some anger had set in.

Maybe my frustration had something to do with my inability to help. I had gone to Africa with the lofty goal of somehow making a difference. I was going home with a life that had been changed forever, but I had little, if any, impact on Africa. At this time it appears that the hidden purpose for this trip was not for me to change Africa, but for Africa to change me.

We had boarded our plane that would take us to Amsterdam. It is almost impossible for me to describe all that was happening while life as I once knew it was being reintroduced.

In the next chapter you will hear about what happened—or, more importantly, didn't happen—on our flight home.

Chapter Forty-Nine

Filled with Purpose

It was 10:00 PM in Amsterdam, and we were boarding the plane that would take us to Chicago. Sometimes a trip seems to fly by, last only minutes, but this one seemed like a lifetime. It was almost as if I couldn't remember where I had come from or how long I had been there. My calendar said ten days, but it really did feel like a lifetime.

I must admit that I was in a very real sense of shock. In a matter of hours, all the people around me had been replaced. There were no longer any physical signs of poverty—no sign of starvation, no shortage of clothes or shoes, and no apparent sickness or disease. All of that had been replaced with air-conditioning, food and soda (with ice), and the freedom to go anywhere or buy anything.

I was feeling a little bit guilty. All the times in my life that I had been unthankful seemed to be flashing before me. All of the things in my life that I had not recognized as blessings were now highlighted and in bold print. I promised to be more thankful for the rest of my life.

I recognized that because of my trip to Africa, I would also have to deal with my frustration with others who had so much, yet complained as if they had so little. If only I could use something from a Star Wars scene and beam them to Africa for an awakening.

On the flight to Chicago, my attention was grabbed by a man three rows ahead of me. There were three seats on each side of the plane and five or six across the middle. This man was in an aisle seat and had two children next to him. Directly across the aisle was a woman that I assumed was his wife.

The lady was always getting up and getting things for him out of the overhead compartment. It was a very long flight, and the overhead compartments were very full. Why would this man just sit there while his wife, or any lady for that matter, continually struggled to get things out of his luggage?

Now I must remind you that I had just seen poverty and abuse that I believe altered my life forever. I somehow had this vision of helping others realize how thankful they should be. I had this feeling of wanting to somehow help families. I envisioned helping dads raise their homes to new levels. We are a country that has so much, yet are often being consumed by our riches. I had this new purpose in life that had been burned into me and could never be erased. I was fresh from battle—very passionate, determined, and hungry to make a difference.

And there, three rows ahead of me, was a husband and father who was too lazy to even get out of his seat to get his own things. He just sat there as his wife rubbed his shoulders and read to him. Man, did he need to hear about my experiences! Did he need to hear about the importance of serving others!

In the next chapters, you will see somebody getting tuned up and see how little it takes to alter the life of another person.

Chapter Fifty

Not as It Seems

About three hours into our flight, I was still focusing on this man, and I thought I had seen it all. The woman and both young children had been serving him the entire time. I thought it was time that I, the person who had just learned so much about serving others, go tell him some things. And just before I was about to get up, something else happened, thankfully!

This man evidently did not have enough privacy, because his wife was putting up a blanket around him. She was using it like a curtain. Then, minutes later, the curtain came down, and his wife went back to her seat.

Shortly following the display that was probably being watched by the entire plane, one of the children decided to leave his seat. The man did not even stand up or get out of his seat to let the child out, but instead made the child crawl over him to get out.

The child headed to the bathroom at the rear of the plane, and moments later, this young child was returning from the bathroom carrying something that completely removed the scales from my eyes. He was carrying a container that I have seen in hospitals to collect urine. As this young boy again crawled across the lap of this man to get to his seat, a chill ran down my spine. His legs were not moving! This man was paralyzed from the waist down! It is true: perception is reality.

This man probably would have given almost anything to be able to get his own things from the overhead compartment. He most likely did not enjoy having to be taken care of, but instead would love to walk, run, and do things for himself. He was not one to be scolded, but instead was someone who—like many of the people in Africa—would teach me so much without saying a word.

There were numerous moments of spiritual revelation during this trip to Africa, and this was another one I would never be able to forget. I could only sit in my seat, motionless and in shock, as this lesson unfolded before me.

Thoughts once again raced through my mind. First, I was thankful that I had not gotten up and scolded this man in front of the entire plane. And then it was as if somebody pushed the pause button on the life of Hank Wagner. It was almost as if a teacher stood in front of me and began to tell me answers to questions, and yet at the same time ask me questions. It was if someone could read my mind and knew exactly what I needed to hear. I did not fight it, or deny it, but like so many other times on this trip, I just got out my notebook and began to write.

Chapter Fifty-One

Can I Love Them?

As I sat on that plane, it was almost as if I could not yet think about home. The experience that had developed out of my judgment of that paralyzed man was not yet over. It was almost as if I was being set up or prepared for some questions that required an open and humble heart.

I am going to share those questions with you, and I would ask that you also be willing to have the same open and humble heart that was required of me. These questions that were asked of me applied to the paralyzed man whom I had just judged. They also applied to the people in Africa that I had just spent part of my life with.

Yet they also apply to many other people, if not all people. I believe that those questions were not only for me to apply to the people of Africa, but to share with others. As you read them, please pause and allow yourself to think of how they might apply in your own life.

Can I love others through their poverty?

Can I love others through the urine in the streets?

Can I love others through the smog-filled air?

Can I love others through the sludge, feces, and urine being dumped in the ocean?

Can I love others through their willingness to be content with what they have?

Can I love others enough to put down my pride and learn from them?

Can I love others enough to give to them, even though it may not be used for what I think is important?

Could I be transparent enough to walk naked down the street and not care what people say (not going to happen, but the question still needs to be asked)?

Would I bathe in a mud hole regularly used by many others to attempt keeping clean?

Could I go to work every day for little or no pay, do my job with primitive tools, and yet be happy?

Could I eat a giant rat and be thankful for it?

Could I watch my child die of starvation and then continue to live myself?

Some of those were some really tough questions for me. And thankfully, hopefully, we will never have to answer them through experiencing them. Maybe it was because I was there and saw some of these things firsthand, but I never go through a day without thinking about them.

Okay, you and I weren't born in Africa, but we could have been. Okay, maybe we can say that we need to be concerned about our own lives and that they are not our problem. I have heard it said, "To whom much is given, much is expected."

I believe it is true: we are expected to use what has been given to us, including what is in us. Each of us has been given much; some don't see it, and some just refuse to believe it. Others choose to not grow or develop all that has been placed in them, for a variety of reasons. And then there are those who realize they have been blessed with gifts, talents, and possessions, but choose to use them only to gain more possessions for themselves. And then there are few who think that all they have is only because of them and what they have done.

I may be wrong, but I think that life is a journey—a journey filled with growth and discovery, a path that can take us almost anywhere and teach us almost anything. Each of our paths will go different places and will contain different experiences and different levels of pain and pleasure. Each of us will be dealt different challenges and presented with different opportunities.

I also believe that all that we have is not for us alone. Many lives are attached to ours, and we are not to be living our life only for us. I am not saying that we should all give away everything that we have and move to Africa. One of my biggest frustrations in Africa was that I could have sold everything that I owned and in a matter of minutes given it all away, yet not positively altered their lives.

We are to be wise with what we have, inside and out. That is part of the high expectations of us, as those who have been given much. If we truly follow our hearts, we will know what to do. We will know if today we are to be quiet, compassionate, or bold. We will know if we are to learn, teach, or give. We will know if we are to simply give a smile or hug. We will know if we are to give words of kindness, compassion, and love, or discernment, correction, and training. We will know if we are to give money or things, and how much. And we will know who to give them to and in what proportion.

I hope that this book has inspired you to be all that you can be. I hope that because of it, you will be more thankful and share more. I pray that your journey is a path that brings constant growth, joy, and abundance for you and all of the lives you touch.

You are important and valuable.

I believe in you.

--------- *Chapter Fifty-Two* ---------

Top Ten

1. Be thankful. I don't care who you are; you have much to be thankful for. Start every day thinking of three things you are thankful for, and it will not only change your day, but also the outcome of your life. And if you want to go another level higher, surround yourself with thankful people.

2. Be careful—the things that you feel, say, and do are contagious. We are all spreading something. Things like joy, happiness, and thankfulness are all contagious. So are the opposite of those. Please help inoculate the rest of the world with the right things—not just by doing, but also by helping others see what you know.

3. Be a leader. Families, our communities, and our world are all crying out for great leaders—leaders who make decisions filtered through integrity and a heartfelt love for others. Someone once told me a great way to help develop world-class leaders. They said, "Take a person out of his/her comfort zone, the more uncomfortable the better, and place them with people they do not know. Out of that experience, a world-class leader will emerge." I do not claim to be a world-class

leader, but my short time in Africa has helped me understand the truth behind that statement.

4. Tests and trials can be good. Many times we think a life without any tests or trials would be great. Yet without them, we would likely never become all that we were meant to be. They not only force us to grow, but they will also give us something that is crucial for any leader, perseverance.

5. Be an answer or solution. We were not created to be a problem. We *all* have gifts and talents that allow us to think and to be creative. We all have resources that are not for us alone. And I am not just talking about our material things, but also the gifts that are within us. We are to use all that we have, both internal and external, to be an answer or a solution.

6. You have a purpose. You were created in this place and at this time not by accident, but for a reason. That purpose will need to not only be discovered, but also grown. You may never have the desire or opportunity to go to a place like Africa, but please, blossom where you are planted. You will not only live a life full of purpose, but this world will be a better place.

7. People are attached to you. It is true—hundreds or maybe even thousands or millions of lives are connected to yours. What will you do with them? How are you currently influencing them? Many of the lives that are connected to us we don't know or will never meet. It may be as simple as another young person seeing how we raise our children. It may be a checkout person who sees our positive attitude. It may be a person on the other side of a crowded parking lot who sees us open the car door for our wives. Some of the people that are connected to us will not even have been born when we leave this planet. Yes, the things we say and do

(both good and bad), to every person, today, may have a huge impact on their lives *and* the generations following them.

8. Find yourself. A magnificent oak tree begins with a tiny acorn. Many things out of its control determine whether it lives or dies. Unlike the oak tree, we can control much of what determines who we are or who we become. Are we who we want to be? If not, we can start today! I went to Africa to give and to somehow make a difference. But Africa did far more for me than I could do for her. This quote best summarizes my trip: "Sometimes you find yourself in the middle of nowhere (Africa), and sometimes in the middle of nowhere you find yourself."

9. You are needed, valuable, special, significant, precious, important, and unique. There has never been another person exactly like you who has ever walked this planet. And there will never be another person just like you ever again on this planet. You were created for this time and for this place. You have purpose and are extremely valuable. Many, many lives are tied to your ability to believe in your significance. Can you believe it? Can you take steps to grow the greatness that is surely within you? I believe you can, and you will.

10. God is real. Hopefully this does not offend anyone. But if you do not know this now, you will. Not only is your eternal destination tied to this truth, but also the outcome of your life on this earth. God created you with a plan and a purpose and knows everything about you. There is a reason why you are here. He knows your purpose, your joys, and your sorrows. If you want to be all that is in you, it will require that you allow your creator to help you. Please don't wait until it is too late to find him.

I love you,
I care about you,
I believe in you.

Printed in the United States
by Baker & Taylor Publisher Services